New 2.75

HOW TO BUY A USED CAR

Charles R. Jackson

HOW TO BUY A USED CAR

Illustrated by George Connelly

CHILTON BOOK COMPANY
Radnor, Pennsylvania

Copyright © 1967 by Charles R. Jackson
First Edition

Second Printing, March 1974

All Rights Reserved

Published in Radnor, Pa. by Chilton Book Company

Library of Congress Catalog Card Number 67-30501

ISBN 0-8019-5292-1
     0-8019-5291-3 (PBK.)

Designed by Edward Coxey

Manufactured in the United States of America.

Contents

1 **This Unique Business**   1
   in which Joe and Harriet buy a used car

2 **Advertising and Dealers**   10
   in which Rogue and Company advertise, and Tiffany and Cartier offer their pearls at low prices

3 **The Best Car for You**   26
   in which a kind word is said for the aristocrats

4 **Used Car Condition and Guarantees**   31
   in which you become the used car reconditioning manager

5 Shopping, Negotiating, Buying   **46**
*in which the dramatic arts
get a workout*

6 Used Car Financing   **61**
*in which Hector V. Throckmorton
buys a car He cannot afford
and is shown the mousehouse technique
and Elmer Gayboy has marital difficulties*

7 A Few Odds and Ends   **84**
*in which we kick around
a few gripes*

1

This Unique Business

in which Joe and Harriet buy a used car

You who intend to buy a used car will do well to own and read this book. And perhaps reread it. It will ensure that when you do buy, you will have a better car than might otherwise have been the case. It is likely, too, that you will save money by being able to make a better deal. It may even immunize you against a serious case of mental distress known as Buyer's Remorse.

This is written with the thought that most people who shop for used cars are not experts on the mechanical condition of automobiles; or gifted in the art of negotiating deals that involve car condition, used car current prices, installment financing, guarantees, taxes, possibly insurance, and plain and fancy horse trading.

This Unique Business

I have a background covering many years as a salesman and sales manager in used car marketing. You can be sure that I know how the market machinery operates; and that I understand customer attitudes and states of mind, including the hope that he will get a good, solid car at a low price. I also realize his apprehension that the car he does buy may just possibly turn out to be not quite as wonderful as the salesman said.

The would-be buyer purchases a used car only once every two, three or four years and can hardly be expected to be an expert with so little practice. He approaches the buying task with many doubts, and rightfully so, for it is widely understood that the whole market has a sort of three-shells-and-a-pea flavor about it. When he actually starts to buy with a respectable amount of his money riding on his decision, he begins to realize that he is something of an amateur; and that as an amateur he must do business with professionals. This guidance from an old "pro" can be helpful.

Before we get down to specifics, the used car market ought to be looked at in the overall. Newspapers and periodicals delight in telling us that this year will be a nine-million-new-car production and sales year. They forecast that ten and twelve-million-new-car production years are soon to come. But they seldom if ever mention that this year's nine-million-new-car sales also mean that twenty two million used cars will be sold—the selling ratio of used to new cars being over 2 to 1. This is a tremendous business nationally; used car sales plus finance charges, sales taxes and motor vehicle fees now total well over $20 billions annually.

Aside from the statistics about the size of the industry

is the human aspect of the business. Half or more of the people who own cars have never bought a new car and it doesn't worry them a bit. The competition for the spendable dollar—the mortgage on the house, house maintenance and improvements, the new TV set, the washer and dryer and new electric refrigerator, the fishing gear and perhaps the boat, the vacation trip—is so tough that a used car is about as far as many people care to reach. Then too, families are more and more becoming two-car families and in the great majority of these cases the second car is a used car. Rather differently situated are the many who cannot afford any but the lowest price cars.

The used car market is very big, and it is unique. There is no other business like it in this country. A major reason is that no two used cars are quite alike; that is, in having the same value. They differ always in the number of miles driven and in maintenance and handling by their respective owners and drivers. There is, for instance, the difference between the "creampuff" previously owned by the Pasadena school teacher who only drove to church on Sundays, lived a mile from the schoolhouse, and never drove after sundown, and the same make and model owned by the lead-footed traveling salesman who poured on 40,000 miles a year in all weather over all types of roads. Obviously, the two cars have widely different values. But on the used car lot they'll look much the same to the shopper. How is he going to tell which is the better car? Don't worry, we'll get to that a little later.

The fact that 90% of car sales involve a trade-in is significant, along with the fact that no two used cars are identical. This immediately brings into the picture a need for negotiation with regard to the trade-in allowance for

This Unique Business

the car being traded. This turns the whole buying and selling process into an operation akin to the haggling customary (and necessary) in an oriental bazaar.

Buyers usually feel that the cars they are trading are worth more than they really are. And they have been educated to believe that they can get a better price than the dealer first quotes for the car they might buy. However, the sellers, "artful dodgers" every one, know this, expect it, and know how to cope with it. Remember, they are the pros in this business and have the operation in a class with the arts, of which acting is not the least.

Some day it may be practical to put a price tag on every used vehicle on the lot and have that price remain the final figure. And it may come about that the trade-in will be conscientiously appraised at its true value, made a part of the deal. When that happy day comes Aunt Agatha can walk in and get the same deal as anyone else. I'm sure that day will come—along about the time that human nature changes completely. But not until then. Meantime, picking the right and best-for-you used car and negotiating the price for the one you buy or the allowance for the one you trade in, and let's not forget the financing which can be tricky and confusing, will continue to be a problem with plenty of pitfalls for the ill-informed or unwary.

In case you doubt that human nature is a major element of the business of buying and selling consider the following, a typical illustration of what both buyers and sellers must contend with. Joe and Harriet go shopping for a used car. At dealer Green's, they find a 1964 Vortex DeLuxe Super, four door, with automatic transmission, power steering, and all the other goodies. Looks pretty sharp. The price is $1,695. It is just about what they have been looking for. So dealer Green's appraiser checks out their old Pumpernickel Special and they are offered $700 for it as a trade-in on the Vortex. However, they continue to shop and at dealer Brown's they find another Vortex DeLuxe that is as like Green's car as two peas in a pod. Of course, no two identical used cars have the same value but for this example we will assume it to be true. Now Brown's Vortex is priced at $1,795. His salesman offers $800 for the old Pumpernickel. Reaction? Joe and Harriet buy from Brown. Remember now, both Green and Brown offered identical cars; the money difference between trade-in allowance and the car price was, in either case, $995. Here is where the human reaction, so basic to this business, comes into play.

Brown's dealership is a great place to do business and Joe and Harriet appreciate that fact and tell their friends about it. Green did not make the sale and if his salesmen cannot handle visitors any better than they have been doing he may still have his 1964 Vortex. You see, Brown sold Joe and Harriet a better car—after all, it had the higher price and so *must* have been better—and this big-hearted dealer recognized and appreciated the excellence of Joe's beloved Pumpernickel and came up with an $800 trade-in offer, all of which proves that he has better judgment and a bigger heart than that Green outfit.

In principle, Dealer Green was right. The $1,695 for his Vortex was a fair selling price while $1,795 for the identical unit on Brown's lot was $100 high. The Green offer of $700 for the Pumpernickel was also in line with the current market. When Brown offered $800 for the Pumpernickel the extra hundred was in the inflated price

This Unique Business

for the Vortex Super he sold. But you'll never convince Joe and Harriet that Brown isn't a better dealer than Green; he sells better cars and gives better trade-in allowances. There was no difference in money between Green's offer and Brown's offer except that the state got the sales tax on an extra hundred in Brown's sale.

I suppose the above case history is acted out one way or another a thousand times a day or more. It serves to illustrate several basic points:

> Joe and Harriet got a good used car of a make and model they wanted in exchange for their car and $995.00 plus tax and transfer of title. It would have been the same if they had bought from Green instead of Brown, except that on Brown's deal they got nicked for that extra three or four dollars in sales tax, not that that's important.
>
> It is important to keep your mind on the cash difference between your trade-in and the car you might buy. If you get carried away with too much enthusiasm for the generous offer for your own Pumpernickel then there can be and probably is inflation in the price of the car to be purchased or, perhaps, shortcomings in the condition of that car, or, inflation in the financing charges—a story reserved for another chapter.
>
> The case shows that, human nature being what it is, dealers just cannot price their used cars on a take it or leave it basis, something like pricing a can of beans in the supermarket. Buyers won't let them. The average buyer has an affection for a car that has served him for two or three years; it is a part of the family just as are the kids and the dog. They are familiar with it; it is a known quantity and they are determined to get all they possibly can for it. Naturally enough, the used car seller

rolls with the punch. He appraises the trade-in at its true value, adds fifty to one hundred or one hundred and fifty to the price of the car he is selling and tacks this on the offer for the trade-in, doing business on that basis. If he doesn't the business goes elsewhere. This situation is not going to change.

At the outset, give more consideration to the condition of the car you are going to buy than to the allowance for your trade. Keep that cash difference figure in mind. When a trade is involved, it helps to consider the purchase just as a "my car and so much money". You'll see the car you are buying and the total cost a little more clearly if your view isn't fogged by the offer on the Pumpernickel you are selling. While you are about it, unless you are in a position to write out a check for the cash difference, find out what the finance charges are going to be; not that the monthly payments are going to be $XY dollars per month for 18 or 24 or 30 months but what you are going to pay in finance charges as a cost of borrowing the money. These charges are part of the price of the car.

One wouldn't ordinarily think so, but if ten persons who have purchased a car in the past six months, or month for that matter, are asked what they paid, eight out of the ten would not be able to say. The whole transaction had become so involved, what with the price of the car, the trade-in allowance, the finance charges, motor vehicle department charges for registration and plates, sales taxes, perhaps insurance, that the usual answer is that they got $725 for their old Mixmaster trade-in and the payments are $58.53 for 24 months—or is it 30 months—they are not sure which. Don't let it bother you. If I had not

This Unique Business

been in the business I wouldn't know either. But you see it does get a little complicated. It does happen somehow that the monthly payment figure which should have been $53.53 became by a little manipulation $58.53. That $5.00 monthly difference doesn't seem to be much but when extended over 24 months it is $120 extra. So—find out what the finance charges are.

In part, the foregoing is what this book is about. It is a guide in making the purchase of a used car simpler and safer.

A few comments about dealers are in order here. New car dealers are automatically in the used car business; and nationwide, there are thousands of independent used car dealers who do not have a new car franchise. Viewing the business as whole, these dealers, new and used car, perform an invaluable service. The market is highly competitive and the efficient dealers have long since found that selling used cars at fair prices as fast as they come in, turning their inventory up to twelve times a year, is far better than holding on to every last unit in an effort to extract the last dime of profit. Nevertheless, let us not overlook the fact that dealers are appropriately named. They are in business to make deals, and deals they do make. Just how good a deal for you depends to considerable extent on your own understanding of the complexities of how the business is conducted.

2

Advertising and Dealers

in which Rogue and Company advertise and Tiffany and Cartier offer their pearls at low prices

Reportedly there are people who walk confidently into new car show rooms, ask a few questions, settle on a certain car, are told the price, and say "I'll take that one. How soon can I get it?" No horsing around. No bargaining. No waste time to talk. That old executive bang, bang! Right now! Frankly, I've met few of these types and when I have it has always been in connection with a new car sale.

Used car buyers arrive at a decision to buy through a sort of slow process that takes about as much time as the breaking up of frost and the coming of spring; that is, unless they have had an accident with their "sled" that makes its immediate replacement imperative. The buying process starts when men, women too, begin to browse through the classified ads on used cars. At first this is just a way to spend a few moments, nothing serious intended; mentally they are only kicking tires. The insidious thing is that sooner or later interest becomes active and they are hooked. Intent to buy becomes firm. Chances are better than 80% that if you are going to buy a used car you will start your shopping at home by reading the ads. Inasmuch as this is a normal preliminary we'll give it attention. Advertisements are not always what they seem—a minority of dealer ads are more notable for what they do *not* say than for what they promise and it will be well, as we shall see, to be able to interpret them. As for ads inserted by private owners, they are mostly inept; honest but inadequate in that they lack appeal and provide insufficient information.

Private-owner ads call for a short discussion, mainly in the interest of the man who is trying to sell his car although the buyer can learn something, too. If you are inserting a classified ad in an effort to sell your 1964 Pumpernickel here are some "do's" and "dont's".

> Do not try to get the job done with the minimum three line ad. You cannot tell enough about the unit to interest anybody; all that can be done with a three-liner is to recite the barest of bare facts. Dealers never use a two or three line ad except within a listing. Yet private sellers seldom spell out their message. If you do not believe me, look at today's paper. Your ad should state you are a private party. Too many just give a phone number leaving it to the reader to infer that the ad has been inserted by a private owner. This leaves the door open for some

Advertising and Dealers

ambitious used car salesman to take a car home over Sunday, put in his ad and wait for calls at his house. You cannot blame a guy for trying. People do like to deal directly with private owners, not considering that usually they won't take trade-ins, want cash, won't help finance, and can give no responsible guarantees.

If you are the original owner, i.e. bought the car new, so state.

Ads inserted by private parties dismiss the engine with a mere "V8". If it is, say, a 390 cu. in. job with a four barrel carburetor say so; this is a high cost option on a popular make and deserves comment.

Too many private ads state "all access". That is not enough. Automatic transmissions, power steering, power brakes, radios, and the like are not accessories, they are options and cost considerable money. If the car has any or all of them, spell it out.

If you know that the mechanical condition of the car is good to excellent don't just say "good". Say "engine, brakes, transmission, all other assemblies, very good". That wording may cost you an extra dollar or more but, remember, you are *selling* this car. Mechanical condition is important to buyers. But don't lie about it.

No trade accepted? Say so and save energy and time.

Possibly 50% of private ads fail to mention color; if they do it is "white" or "blue", or some other. People are color conscious; if the man isn't his wife is. Put some appeal in the ad. Note that no manufacturer sells white cars—they are "Coventry White" (whatever that is), or "Mediterranean Blue" or "Forest Green". "Coal Mine Ebony" if we want to stretch a point. If the finish on your car is excellent use the manufacturer's name for it if you can remember, such as "Indian Summer Gold"; if you cannot remember, name the color, you have as much license to do this as the factory copywriter.

In the essence, the whole idea is to make strangers who have never seen you or your car want to buy it. Your ad is competing with dozens or scores of other ads. Give it some distinction, give it appeal, make it informative and you'll sell yours while other private advertisers are waiting for the phone to ring.

Now what does the ad cost? The city newspaper in this area reaches well over half a million people. They charge $6.75 for a three line ad, $13.50 for a six line ad, $18.00 for an eight line ad; this is for five days but they'll run the ad for eight days if the advertiser doesn't call to cancel when he has sold the car. As between the three liner and the six liner the spread is $6.75, little to pay to ensure a sale and that at the best price. Borrow the technique used by the professionals.

Now we come to dealer advertisements. Most of these are straightforward; some of the ads are really informative although the large display type ads are often merely simple listings of ten to fifteen units. As to prices it is a bit difficult to generalize. A few dealers seem to have no hesitancy about quoting prices that are on the high side, very much so. While this seems self-defeating it does have the merit of leaving room to maneuver on price when the deal is being negotiated and, after all, the average used car buyer does not know much about current prices anyway. If he knows the price is high with respect to the current market, he is apt to think that the car is much better than average.

However, most dealers sharpen their pencils on the

Advertising and Dealers

price of five or ten cars that they are advertising, and will state that forty other used cars are in stock and let it go at that, leaving the impression that all other prices are in line with those quoted.

When the dealer really puts in a hullabaloo about his special sale you can assume that it really is a sale *of the cars advertised only* and prices on these are low. Also, you are not going to get a generous offer for your trade-in.

I am sorry to say that on many big volume used car lots some of the salesmen will deliberately disregard newspaper advertisements inserted by their own dealership when these ads feature certain cars. Let's say the ad states "was $1,395 now marked down to $1,195 for quick sale. Hurry." The price cut is severe but having had the unit on the lot for six, eight or ten weeks it is now time to get rid of it. Assume that a shopper arrives who has not seen the ad. The boys who play rough, and there are more than a few, start dealing on the old price of $1,395. If the customer buys, perhaps at a figure well over the $1,195 quoted in the advertisement, that's the deal and that is the way it stays. Does the sales manager revise the figure and paperwork? Not jolly well likely. If, however, the shopper, having seen the paper and identified the car advertised, directs the attention of the salesman to the error of quoting $1,395 or some other high figure, there is an appropriate display of astonishment about the misquote, the customer is congratulated on being able to get that $1,395 job for a $200 cut-price, and they start over on the new basis. Big operations run big ads in the classified columns with considerable frequency—strange, how much less frequently is the ad, clipped from the paper, to be found tacked to the wall in the show room or closing

How To Buy A Used Car

room and there exposed to public gaze. An oversight? Could be. Maybe not though, maybe not.

In the bad old days some of the wheeler-dealer advertisements offered non-existent cars for sale, dreamboat quality at very low prices. The idea was to create traffic on the used car lot. When buyers arrived they were informed the advertised car had been sold. The basis of the gimmick was that visitors drawn by the ad were certainly in the market and could be shown other cars—these *not* at giveaway prices. This advertising of imaginary cars was stopped by the city newspapers who, acting as a group, required all advertisers to insert in each ad the identifying number of the car or cars they were advertising. This made it simple to check the matter since the dealer inventory accounts would show appropriate entries, as would dealer reports (to the Motor Vehicle Dept.) of sales made and dates of sale. The penalty for trying to beat the requirement was refusal by any paper in town to accept the advertisements of the culprit, this being enough to put offenders practically out of business. Ethical dealers planned and inspired this action in order to protect themselves from grossly unfair competition and, incidentally, by doing so they also protected the public. It is a good example of businessmen in a community effectively cleaning up a malpractice without running to city or state authorities.

The following advertisements appeared in the past two days in our local Daily Astonisher-News. They are quoted as examples of ads that require interpretation. They are telling just part of a story, leaving much that is unsaid.

Advertising and Dealers

CHECK THESE BARGAINS
NO CASH NEEDED, 100% FINANCING—All Cars Carry a One Year or 50,000 Mile Warranty on parts and labor.
(This is followed by a listing of ten cars at very low prices)
YOUR TRADE ACCEPTED PAID FOR OR NOT

Ripley could have run this one in his "Believe It Or Not" series. No cash needed? 100% financing? This ad will create traffic on the used car lot but visitors are certain to find that unless their credit is absolutely gilt-edged they are going to need some down payment or collateral —perhaps a chattel on their furniture.

The one year or 50,000 mile warranty verges on the absurd. The standard translation means that it is one year or 50,000 miles, whichever comes first. If the ad said 20,000 miles it would be a little more sensible in this respect—one would almost have to live in the car to do 50,000 miles in one year. However, the important element is: what does the warranty offer? Is it a 15% discount on parts and labor? You guess.

Your trade accepted paid for or not? People who try to trade off unpaid-for cars are not, in general, good credit risks. Do you think the dealer is going to sell his cars without some down payment or other security? (You can believe that he will ask, "How much is the dining room and bedroom furniture worth?")

PAY ONLY $2 TRANSFER FEE
AND ASSUME BALANCE
JOHN DOE AUTO SALES, INC.

This is a come-on. The implication is that the advertiser has repossessed cars and the buyer can have them at bargain prices. As will be related later there is rarely such a thing as a repossession at a bargain to the general public. Forget it.

The same page of the newspaper shows another ad stating:

REPOSSESSION

and goes on to describe the car in detail. It says the outstanding balance is $768.21 and the payments will be $26.96 per month. Any transfer of title will require payment of sales tax. Has this item been added to the outstanding balance, assuming that it is a bonafide repossession? If so, what other charges have been added; for instance work orders covering tires, battery, lot charge for general clean-up, and so on? Dealer profit perhaps? Will the dealer sell the car without a down payment? His ad does not say so, it merely states that the outstanding balance is $768.21 and can be paid off at $26.96 per month. The ad may create a lot of traffic; those who are drawn to the lot will learn the rest of the story when they get there; quite a bit has been left unsaid.

Any number of ads describe cars and promote a myth by stating "Pay Only $25 Salesman's Fee and Assume Balance of $XY per month". By implication the cars are repossessions—most unlikely. The same jokers run the same type of ads day after day, week after week, and there just are not that many repos. Missing from ad information is the full price of the car, all they say is that the balance outstanding is so much and payments are so much per month. How many months? There is a finance clobber in this and you can bet the payments will run for enough months to yield a profitable selling price plus a usurious profit on the finance charge. This, though, is a tactic that must sell cars since the ads are consistent, variations appearing daily.

Advertising and Dealers

Ethical new car dealers, and they are in the majority, do not run ads along the come-on lines highlighted above. Their ads on used cars may be simple listings; sometimes they do a good job of describing the car, presenting the selling price of the unit and stating the minimum down payment. As I write I have several examples in front of me.

Here is an ad, same date, same paper, from a good dealer. I don't know him personally but have a fellow feeling for the used car manager, who works at his job. The ad lists sixteen cars (this is a big dealer and I assume they have not less than fifty used units in stock) each of them being given treatment similar to the following:

'65 HORNET CONVERTIBLE

"This 235 horsepower V8 honey sports a gleaming red coat, four-on-the-floor shift, power steering, radio, heater, and whitewall tires. You simply can't go wrong at $2,395 or only $300 down plus sales tax and license and $68.66 per month."

Comment: The down payment will actually be over $400 since to the $300 mentioned in the ad there must be added $95.80 sales tax (at 4% of $2,395) plus transfer of title. But, Lord knows the dealer doesn't get any part of the sales tax or motor vehicle department fees. The ad wording is legitimate. And good, it tells the story. Does not say the number of monthly payments but my pencil tells me it is 36.

From another dealer, big and legitimate, same paper and date:

'62 $1495

"Hooper's luxury four door model. This fine road car is finished in popular white with a dark beige interior. For the utmost comfort and roominess here it is. Plan on

How To Buy A Used Car

unexpected driving pleasure at a very low price".

Comment: Plenty of romance but not much information. Sedan or Hard Top? Mechanical condition? Mileage? Down payment? Undoubtedly this car has power brakes, power steering, probably electric windows and seat but you'd never know it from the ad.

Now that you have looked over the ads the next logical step is to go shopping. Where to go? We all know that new car dealers are automatically in the used car business. As is usual, in nine cases out of ten they must take a trade-in on a new car sale, then sell the trade and possibly take a second trade, then perhaps a third trade for a washout. And of course there are the independent used car dealers who have no new car franchise. Let's examine the situation.

The location of the new car dealership has a bearing. Every city has areas and suburbs where the general run of residents have a substantially higher-than-average income. These areas make a happy hunting ground for used car buyers. Beverly Hills, California, is an excellent example. It is noted for its high median income and is a city entirely surrounded by metropolitan Los Angeles. (There, new car sales in proportion to used car sales are out of balance; there is a relatively much stronger demand for new cars than for used cars than is normal.) New car sales bring in trades and as the market for used cars is slow the dealers have a harder time moving them. The factories keep putting on pressure to sell more and more new cars; the dealers cannot afford to permit incoming trades to accumulate so they price them attractively, making them good buys. They must also wholesale many

Advertising and Dealers

units to independent used car operators in other sections of the city.

In addition to price attraction, used cars available in the high-income areas tend to be of good quality. Affluent owners will have spent whatever is necessary to keep them well maintained. Dealer used car inventories average a high percentage of late model cars since the public will trade frequently just to keep abreast of the newest models. Do not overlook the high income area when you shop. Quality may be higher and prices lower than you may have thought. I suspect that many buyers shrug off the high income areas as unsuitable locales to shop for used cars being under the impression that prices there must be in line with Tiffany jewels, or pearls from Black, Starr and Frost. Not so, dear reader, not so!

The independent dealers are the real pros in this business. And they are truly expert. They have no new car franchise and, in contrast to many new car dealers who moan about their used car operation, they like the used car business and are in it for fun, games and profit. Many are good dealers in the sense that they are good people to do business with. At the same time more than a few are so slick that they can go into a revolving door after you and come out in front. Since the independent dealers, and the new car dealers for that matter, do not go along with the TV dictum that the good guys wear white hats and the bad guys wear black hats, there isn't a positive way to know which is which—good guy or bad guy?

Most likely, a good dealer will have been in business for a considerable period. The people to whom he has sold cars have been pleased with the treatment they have received, they have told friends, and when again in the market former customers have come back for another car. Size and continuity are measures of service. Used car customers are a loyal lot when they have been well served.

In the main, the independent gets his cars, at wholesale, either directly from new car dealers or via wholesale auctions. They buy a few from private owners. And of course they too must take trades on cars they sell and must liquidate the trades. Many specialize in high priced cars that are status symbols, or in station wagons, or convertibles, or in cheapies of which more later.

Where will the independents be located? We discussed the high-income area in which used cars have relatively light demand. A reverse situation exists in the low-income area. There, the heavy demand is for used cars and in consequence used car independents tend to establish their selling activities in industrial sections or wherever the median income is low—on the wrong side of the tracks, so to speak. This is not the case for the dealer who specializes in the high-priced status symbol cars and buys them at wholesale auctions anywhere within a radius of 500 miles or more, or for the specialists in station wagons and late model convertibles. However, it is true in general.

The average buyer in the low-income area is more vulnerable to sleight-of-hand and the fast shuffle in connection with finance; his monthly payments can turn out to be really loaded. His attention will be focused by the salesman on the high trade-in allowance he may be offered (after considerable negotiation) or a cut in the original asking price of the car he is interested in buying (the asking price, as usual, having been high to allow for an over-

Advertising and Dealers

allowance on the trade or for a price cut.) A surprisingly large number of buyers will sign orders without knowing what the total cost of the transaction will be—this is especially true in the low-income areas where customers are keenly aware that they can stand payments of, say, $49.50 a month but not $65.00 a month. Never mind how many months. The sharpies in the business get fat on this one. Happy with the car, content that he can make the $49.50 monthly payments, Rufus takes off pridefully to impress his friends with his new set of wheels, to have a beer, and let the future take care of itself. He knows how much the individual monthly payment will be, possibly knows how many months of payments, but does not bother to multiply one by the other. His $49.50 per month times 24 months is $1,188 which he is paying for a car worth $800 on which he has traded his old "sled" for a $225 down payment.

Want my recommendation? Buy your used car from a franchised new car dealer. He is in the used car business because he must be—it is an inevitable part of his operation. Not that new car salesmen cannot or do not throw a punch below the belt on occasion for they can and often do. But the new car factory is doing its best to see to it that the dealer is running a creditable operation and is an effective representative. The factory presses him to sell those used cars at retail if he can, or wholesale if he must—but move them. The result is that these dealers, on cars that have been around a little too long, will price them to move. And they are not quite so apt to gimmick the financing.

I will say this: the average independent used car dealer knows his used car business better, or at least gives it more

How To Buy A Used Car

efficient management, than the average new car dealer knows and manages his own used car operation. Fat, dumb and happy after a succession of profitable years of new car sales too many dealers will turn over management of the used car operation to some joker whose single asset may be that he is a good closer, that is, a leading salesman who can help other salesmen close their deals. Superb con-men and persuasive talkers, these types are seldom real managers, interested in car condition, willing to analyse inventory unit by unit to see which cars have been around too long and why they haven't sold in a reasonable period.

Quite a bit has been said about dealerships; we might comment about dealers as people. As individuals they are as good outgoing citizens as one can hope to find in any field of commerce. Indeed, I recall one who spent so much of his time and effort being on the Board of Governors of the Children's Hospital and as Director of the Community Chest Drive and on the City Commission and the Board of the Country Club that he had little time left over. Came a period when sales slipped badly and he had to be warned to take a more intensive interest in operating his business. He was being outclassed by the competition.

However, as good citizens as dealers may be in community affairs, they have an eye for the balance sheet, the profit and loss statement, and are aware they cannot give cars away and survive, regardless of what Madman Muntz used to say many years ago. Some of you must remember that advertising: "I'd give 'em away but my wife won't let me". It just isn't so.

This is a dealing business run by dealers. The transactions are 90% those in which a questionable commodity,

Advertising and Dealers

your car (plus money) is swapped for another questionable commodity, the dealer's car. However, the rewarding thing about it is that one can get for $1,895 a car that sold originally for $4,000, and that $4,000-baby will still have almost all of the performance and looks and smooth riding it had when it was new. You can if you know how to go about buying it. If one doesn't know how to go about buying it, and is a little unlucky, it is possible to wind up with that case of buyers remorse we were talking about a little while back.

3

The Best Car for You

*in which a kind word
is said for the aristocrats*

What is the best car for you? Before shopping, make up your mind as to the body type for which you have a preference—four-door sedan or four-door hardtop, or station wagon, or whatever—and the general price bracket. This matter may seem too elementary to be worth mentioning but the number of people is surprising who go shopping and seem unable to say what they want. Women in general are more sensible than men in this respect, and at the same time a little more difficult. They will state flatly that they want a good car for about $1,000 (and a good thing, too) without seeming to care whether they get a convertible or a station wagon, or any particular make. It is not until later that the dealer learns that their idea of a $1,000-car is a unit that would normally bring $1,800, and that they cannot abide grey but love rose-pink or fuchsia.

You may have a decided preference for a certain make. Say so. But don't make too big an issue of it; this could foreclose you from being shown a "creampuff" of another make in just the right body type, color, condition, and price range that you are looking for. The salesman could know of recent arrivals that are in the shop being conditioned for sale; at the morning sales meeting he may have been informed as to other units due to come in as trades.

Let's say that there is no especial preference for make or model. The car may be wanted as a second car for the family. If so, it might be well to give some consideration to buying one of the luxury, originally high-priced cars. There are several reasons for this. These are cars that when new sold for $6,000 and more. Today all cars, even the least expensive, are built to operate for at least ten years and a minimum life of well over 100,000 miles. However, as a second car the luxury units have much to recommend them.

In general they are in good condition. The original owners paid a high price for them. In the main this type of car is purchased, when new, by citizens in the better-than-average income bracket. They are almost certain to have been sufficiently responsible to see to it that proper preventive maintenance servicing was performed—used the best oil and premium gasoline, had periodic lubrication, and oil and filter changes whenever necessary—and were not obsessed like the dragsters with the idea of beating everyone else away from the stop signal or taking corners

The Best Car for You

on two wheels. On this type of car 35,000 miles is just a break-in period. You can be proud to own and drive one of these aristocrats.

As to price? Original owners expect to take a fairly severe depreciation on them, downwards from the original high cost. One result is that they keep them longer and a five year old car on the lot may have had only one owner, which is not likely to be true for cars of the popular price class. Result—prices for these beauties when four to five years old are little higher than prices for cars of the same year in makes that sold for $2,000 less when new. One of the reasons for this price decline is a widespread belief that a high cost of operation makes them just too expensive to own and drive. Not necessarily. They cost no more to lube or wash or park than any of the others. As to insurance the big end is for property damage and public liability coverage (PL & PD) and this costs no more. Fire and theft coverage is the same. There is an increase in collision coverage cost but not too much. Cost of gasoline has been given too much emphasis—expense for fuel should not increase over a dollar or so a week unless a lot of miles are being driven. And, after all, look at what you are getting. Also, points and sparkplugs and fan belts cost little more and with these beautifully engineered and carefully assembled units there is not so great a possibility of engine, transmission or rear end trouble.

These aristocrats usually have all the accessories, including air conditioning. They are no problem for the woman driver because they always have power steering and power brakes. Being big they are safer. On that last item, national safety statistics on automobile accidents give the big car an edge over the little car.

How To Buy A Used Car

You can see that I have my prejudices when it comes to luxury cars. Differ if you choose. One more comment though about this matter of fuel consumption. The producers of the popular price makes are coming out with engines that are close to and sometimes over the 425 cu. in. range, having high compression heads and four-barrel carburetors. These engines are usually extra-cost options in the higher priced models. They can use gas in gallons equivalent to those used by the engines in cars having a cost when new of over $6,000.

4

Used Car Condition and Guarantees

*in which you become
the used car
reconditioning manager*

The mechanical condition of used cars offered for sale is a subject on which I am touchy. There are widespread, chronic abuses in the industry that somehow need to be overcome. Out of the 22 million used cars that will be sold this year a significant percentage will be unsafe to operate—how many I do not know nor do I believe anybody else knows either. But it will be too many whatever the number. Some states, and it should be all of them, enforce mandatory periodic inspections of the mechanical condition of *all* operating motor vehicles in connection with safety features, i.e., brakes, lights, turn indicators, and windshields and glass for all around vision. Brakes include parking as well as foot brakes; glass includes not only

Used Car Condition and Guarantees

replacement of broken or frosted glass but the provision of adequate rear view mirrors. Deficiencies are noted during inspection and the car is not cleared for continued operation unless shortcomings are corrected within a specified period of time, usually a week. However, these inspections apply to the general public and not to the car dealers. Of this, more later.

Now let us assume that *you* are the dealer. How much are you going to spend and to what extent will you go to condition for sale the cars you are taking in trades? I can tell you. Unless you are the exception, you'll spend most of your effort and money on appearance reconditioning. It is what the public sees. It makes the car attractive. It sells cars. You would have fender dings ironed out. You would have the badly cracked glass on the left rear door replaced, put in a new front floor mat if the old one is too worn, perhaps even replace the rubber pad on the foot brake. With a little paint touch-up, chrome polish, shampoo and a wax job the car will sparkle. It is ready for the front line.

But you wouldn't do much about mechanical repair or rebuilding. The reason is simple—the public just will not pay for extensive mechanical reconditioning. Quite the contrary, if informed that a new set of piston rings has been installed a buyer is apt to get the idea the car is worn out (although it may be far from it) and shy away. This is so much the fact that many a car emitting heavy blue smoke from the exhaust, an oil burner and traded for that reason, has had a set of good piston rings and bearings installed by the dealer but the buyers are seldom advised of it. The rings should handle the problem for the next 20,000 to 30,000 miles, possibly more, and the buyer is getting a bonus. However, the dealer will not do this work unless he must. He knows that the blue smoke is a giveaway that would make the car unsaleable to alert buyers, and that to inform a buyer that the car had had a ring job would scare him off, although it shouldn't. In the end, as an experienced dealer you would proceed on the premise that if the car needs extensive mechanical work it is better to move it off the lot at a low price and let the customer be the judge of the work needed. He could then have this performed to the extent he desired, at a place of his own choice, spending as much or as little as he cared to.

The scene changes. You are no longer a dealer or used car reconditioning shop manager. You have become a prospective buyer. To your eyes, cars that have been expertly appearance-conditioned, even though in sorry shape mechanically, have allure and appear as desirable as other used cars, of the same year and make, that are mechanically in top shape. Not being an auto appraiser, and these experts can be led astray too on occasion, and with no real training in automobile mechanics how are you going to determine which cars are sound? In part, rely on the reputation of the dealership. When shopping insist, and I do mean insist, that the prime consideration is that the car must be in top condition mechanically—we will get into this shopping detail soon.

In fairness I must say that over the years, indeed, for the past three decades to my own knowledge, the car manufacturers have spent much money and manpower in programs designed to guide their dealers in this matter of reconditioning used cars for sale. They want most sincerely to see their dealers do the job right and establish reputations for fair and just dealing. It is in the factory

Used Car Condition and Guarantees

interest that this be so—the dealer must sell the trades to make room for more and more trades on new cars. Too, the reputation of a dealer in his community has much to do with his success, or lack of it, as an effective representative for his factory.

Nonetheless, the factory also knows that any dealer who tries to overhaul or rebuild every used unit he handles is going to wind up broke. It is one of the reasons for a big wholesale traffic in used cars, for many dealers will not mess around with retailing trades that are not reasonably high level. Many, many perfectly sound cars are wholesaled by dealers when they are overstocked or for some other good and sufficient reason. But back to the point of overdoing this overhaul matter: I knew a dealer in Arizona who took a lease on an old barn on the edge of town for the purpose of all-out reconditioning of his used cars. He hoped to sell units so sound mechanically that, in time, his pre-eminence would be firmly established, benefiting his new car sales inasmuch as moving his trades would become simple. It didn't work. His competition killed him off so to speak for (and here is that human nature thing again) people did not want to know that the cars had been overhauled and were attracted more by price incentive, hoping to get a solid car for the low buck. A lot of them did of course; and I suspect that some were sadly disappointed. So there we are.

This question of car condition, and what the buyer is to do to cope with it, is difficult to resolve. Ask the salesman? Yes—this is automatic and inevitable. You can be sure the salesman, if he is really trying to sell you a specific car, is going to tell you all the nice things he knows about the unit if he knows anything at all about its history. And you can be equally sure he is not going to tell you anything he may happen to know that may be unfavorable. True, many salesmen get cold on cars they do not like and just refuse to show them. For some this is a tribute to their moral virtue and sterling character. But for most it is simply because they have fired up a succession of prospects, made demonstrations and spent much effort in trying to sell them, only to have doubting prospects walk away. The bad reaction is usually the result of poor performance as a result of unsatisfactory mechanical condition. The unit becomes a semi-permanent boarder on the lot, reaches the 30, 60 and 90-day mark as a non-paying guest for the lot hostler to keep tinkering with, and the dealer would be well advised to dump it wholesale or retail, no guarantee, at a low, low price, and to take his lumps on this one as all dealers must from time to time.

But back to the salesman. We've already said that this is a horse-trading type of operation implying that it is the inheritor of the traditions of the old time horse swappers who in forty years of trading handled only horses that were sound in wind and limb, young, strong and willing, with no bad habits. (I wonder who it could have been who handled horses that were spavined, or just plain dangerous to be around.) Used car salesmen are almost invariably on a commission basis; they receive a percentage of the gross profit on the sale. It is asking too much of human nature to expect them to be utterly candid about their merchandise, to tell the whole truth and nothing but the truth, at all times, to all and sundry. So don't expect it. They satisfy the conventions of the business by telling the good things about the rig. As a protective measure a good many resolve the problem for themselves by refusing to

Used Car Condition and Guarantees

waste time on cars in which they have no faith. They, and I have been among them, just blandly announce they do not like the car the prospect is looking over, wouldn't sell it, and gently steer the buyer to another car.

As to this car-condition question:

> If the salesman tells you it is a one-owner car, sold by the firm originally and serviced by them, the action is simple. Go to the service department and have them pull the customer service file jacket on the car. This will show what work has been done and the work orders will show mileage.
>
> If the price of the car is substantial, say $1,895 (there has never been a $1,900 price in the history of the business and it appears to be illegal to price used cars other than at figures ending in $—95 or $—45) and if you are in doubt and are serious about buying the unit ask if you can take it to your favorite repair shop for inspection. Any dealer will go along with this. For a small charge your shop will pull off one or two wheels to inspect brakes and brake drums, give the steering a once-over, inspect for indications of collision, check the engine and transmission. It's a small cost to you for objective professional advice on mechanical condition, especially when you may be investing over $2,000, or less for that matter.

Of course the dealer guarantee, or warranty if you prefer that term, is solely concerned with the condition of the car. It is intended to set the buyer's mind at rest about this matter, to protect, to ensure that should mechanical troubles develop through no fault of the driver that the dealer will come to his aid. Do the guarantees or warranties protect? A lot of them do. And some of them promise much but protect little.

How To Buy A Used Car

The car manufacturers have excellent guarantees on their new cars and these are transferable to owners who buy the car after it has passed from the hands of the man who bought it as a new car, provided: the first and subsequent owner/drivers have certain periodic servicing work performed, and the car is within the mileage or time limitations of the guarantee. Starting with the 1967 year model all motor manufacturers provide a 50,000 mile or five year (whichever comes first) warranty on the power train; that is, on the engine, transmission drive line, differential (rear axle and gears) and related parts and sub-assemblies in the event of failure due to defects in materials or workmanship originating with the manufacturer. The warranties include labor as well as parts but do not cover consumables such as tires, ignition points and spark plugs, brake lining, fan and generator belts, and other high-mortality items. Nor should they. Since the dealer pays for what must be done, with the factory reimbursing him for his out-of-pocket cost, there is little argument from the dealer as to whether he will live up to the terms of the factory warranty. He will. If the case is marginal the car owner will get the benefit of a doubt. Plain evidence of abuse or neglect, such as operating with insufficient oil or water, overloading beyond capacity or operating over shattering terrain, will void the warranty just as will failure to observe the required periodic servicing steps called for in the warranty. In the case of one manufacturer the record of periodic servicing is sent to the appropriate regional office of the factory—reasonable enough since it is the factory that must pay the costs of warranty claims—and the dealer cannot certify the transfer of warranty to a second or third owner until the factory gives

Used Car Condition and Guarantees

clearance to do so. This prevents any hanky-panky with regard to mileage driven or preventive maintenance. In the main, buying a car that is still within the warranty period is good protection for the buyer.

Not too many can buy used cars still within the warranty period. The bulk of the used units sold this year will be beyond warranty mileage or age. If you find one, it is important to know what the dealer warranty covers.

If the car has been well maintained and the dealer knows it, if it is that famous Pasadena school teacher's car for instance, the dealer may give you a 100% guarantee on parts and labor for a matter of months. Good. Trouble is that so many used cars may pass through the hands of a dealer in a month, even in a medium sized operation, that under present methods of dealer operation and lack of reconditioning policy it is practically impossible for all concerned actually to know when a well-nigh perfect car is front-lined for sale. After they have been given a mild tune-up and appearance-conditioned almost all used cars run well and look lovely.

There is a considerable difference between warranties on used cars. Some say what they mean in explicit terms and the advertisements do not mislead. Others give little protection and it is not difficult for a dealer to advertise that his selected used cars being offered in this ad are all protected by a one-year or two-year guarantee or warranty. It's up to the buyer to find out what the terms of the protection really are.

The 50-50 guarantee is almost a standard of the industry. It is fair to both the buyer and to the seller. It changes from time to time, always becoming more liberal but in general it warrants that during the first 1,000 (or

2,000) miles of driving, or first month (or two months) after delivery of the car, whichever comes first, the dealer and the customer will split, on a 50-50 basis, the costs of any necessary repairs. Dealers can well afford this and usually offer it cheerfully. The work *must* be done in his dealership. However, don't expect it on cars that are too old or too cheap. The dealer has an edge here; he buys his parts at a discount and pays his mechanics 50% of retail labor charges so his out-of-pocket costs are not great. Still, work done under these guarantees does cost him money and can crowd profitable service business out of his service department. Some of the 50-50s carry an additional offer of a 15% discount on parts for 24 months or 24,000 miles—this is a bonus.

On the other hand there are guarantees or warranties that are mentioned in the advertising as being good for one year or two years. An imposing warranty card will be given the used car buyer. Spelled out, it states that umpteen hundred car dealers in several states will recognize the card and will give a 15% discount on parts for the next two years. The discount may be worth something but it is evident that this warranty is more of a sales technique than a real protection. If a buyer is about to settle for a used car with a dealership that offers this 15% discount on parts and nothing more, he would be prudent to insist that whatever protection he thinks the car should have be written on the face of the order form before he signs it. Vague promises don't mean much. They are far from ironclad and there is always some joker in a position of authority in the dealership who can say "no" in positive terms.

While on the subject of guarantees it must be pointed

Used Car Condition and Guarantees

out that batteries, tires, glass and sundry other items are exempt from coverage. These exemptions are in the fine print on the guarantee document and are usually not noted until a need for related service is discovered. Don't blame the dealer. It can be stated with conviction that if this protection (for the dealer) were not there the result would be an open invitation for the customer to return within a short period for new tires, or a new battery and electrical parts, or a new right rear door glass (broken by the customer's son Roger) two weeks after delivery.

I must say that as a sales manager I learned early to point out to a complaining customer, showing him the fine print, that his warranty did not cover the battery or tires; and then, often, to suggest that we have a new or rebuilt battery installed for him, or a recap tire mounted. The cost to the dealership would always be less than $20 and usually nearer $10. This action would win for the dealership, at least with this man, an image of being a good place to do business, run by nice guys. With the gift would go the implication that in return for the battery or tire, it would be nice if the customer would bring us a new customer. Naturally, if he appreciated good treatment he ought to be glad to have his friends come to see us when in the market. People respond to this sort of thing extremely well and bring in friends practically by the hand. This type of customer relations is inexpensive and rewarding and I cannot understand why some used car managers will not yield on minor warranty points in order to gain the greater benefit. They ought, instead, to welcome an opportunity to add unpaid, enthusiastic sales representatives to their staffs. The cost is small and can be written off against advertising. I suppose that many managers become a little cynical about customers returning for service to which they have no legal right, but there is a moral obligation surely when business has been done in good faith. And of this I am certain—people have themselves become cynical about used car selling and when they find an outfit that will treat them with consideration, particularly in the matter of after-service, they become fiercely loyal. They *do* bring in their friends, they *do* send people to the lot.

Mechanical condition is a hard one to cover. People do expect, or at least hope, that when they spend $1,495 for a used car they will get one that is safe to operate and that is in good enough running condition to give them thousands of miles of trouble free operation. I would like to see used car conditioning routines established that would result in the dealer being able to put a window sticker on the car certifying that the brake system had been inspected and serviced for operation, that there had been an engine analyser test and tune-up, and that the exhaust system, lights and turn signals, steering and tires were in condition to pass any legal safety inspection. The public deserves this protection. Dealers would bear the cost but this would not be so great as to stop them. You, the buyer, would then be able to approach any used car lot with confidence. But this is too much to hope for. You must try to cope with the situation as it is.

Here are indications that tell-tale used car condition: Today's factory paint jobs are so good that a car will rarely need a repaint until it is at least five years old, usually older. If a three-year-old unit has practically new paint, and I don't mean a spot job on a fender or trunk lid, the indication may be that there had been a collision

Used Car Condition and Guarantees

that could have thrown the frame out of line or had other serious consequences. Lift the hood and look at the fire wall. That's the wall between the engine compartment and the driver's seat. This is so covered with ignition harness wiring and other gear that it is not practicable to dismantle the attachments to permit repainting the wall and therefore it will be the original color. It should tell you if the car has been repainted.

Is a lot of dark or light blue smoke (not white steam which is just warm moist air on a cold day) coming out of the exhaust tailpipe after the engine has been running for three or four minutes? This could indicate high oil consumption. The car may need a piston ring job, or an engine rebuild.

Buying a station wagon? You find one two years old that looks like a dandy. Make an extra effort to find out its history of operation. If a suburban family owned it, fine; buy it. But station wagons cost like crazy when new and not many families trade them when only two years old. The fact is, they are scarce in the used car market. It could be that the wagon was used for newspaper distribution—out at 3:30 every morning with a half ton of papers, making 150 miles a day with frequent cowboy starts and stops dropping off 20 lbs. of papers here and 50 lbs. there. Or it could be some other high-mileage commercial operation. Station wagons are the traveling man's friend. Try to find out. Don't let this discourage you on station wagons—they are bargains considering their original price. But be a little cautious.

Check the underbody trim of any car for extensive rust or corrosion. Practically all city streets and main highways in areas subject to winter's snow and ice are heavily salted, and salt is corrosive. The car manufacturers have done wonders in the past decade in devising means to overcome the inevitable rust. They treat exposed under-surfaces chemically, and dealers in these areas will seldom deliver a new car without undercoating. Still, while the situation is far better than it was years ago, rust may be a real problem. Take a look, especially if the car is five years or more old. The Pacific coast and southern states are happily spared this problem almost altogether.

Are new seat covers on the car you are looking at? This could be dealer consciousness of the importance of appearance conditioning. Take a look at the headlining (overhead upholstery). If this is shabby, dirty, and torn in places then suspect the reason for the new seat covers. The other side of this coin is that lots of careful people put seat covers on their beautiful new upholstery within a week or so after they have taken delivery of their new car—the new seat covers on the car on the used car lot may just be replacements for the first set and the upholstery under them as fresh as when it was new three years ago. Take a look also at the upholstery under the seat covers.

Can you rely on the used car salesman to tell you all you should know about the car in connection with mileage, condition of engine, brakes, and so on? Not by a long shot! In the first place he probably knows very little about its mechanical condition, unless it's poor. (In this connection, I exempt dealers in small towns where everyone seems to know everyone else. The dealer himself may be making the decisions on conditioning of the used cars he takes in trades. Business is on a more personal basis with people one has known for years. I feel that the small town dealer

Used Car Condition and Guarantees

is able to give better personal management and supervision and will go farther in this conditioning matter.)

Since mechanical condition is so important, if you have any doubts about this aspect of a car under consideration, take it to your neighborhood repair man for his examination. Don't tell him where you got it. Do tell him you may buy it. After all, a respectable amount of your money is riding on his answer.

Never conclude a deal without learning what guarantee goes along with the car being purchased. Get a 100% guarantee if you can. Take the 50-50 guarantee if that is house policy—it is a fair guarantee for both customer and dealer. Recognize the fact that used cars are not new cars. Good used cars in the upper and medium price brackets should give years of faithful service. Do not forget, you are buying a car for from $1,000 to $1,500 or more off the price of the unit when new.

Your or your mechanic's inspection of the car should not overlook the tires—one of the most obvious indications of wear and tear. Your safety depends upon sound tires. Insist on replacements if the tires are too slick, or have cracked or cut sidewalls. Or, be prepared to replace them yourself.

In any case, don't rely on the speedometer reading to tell you how far the car has travelled. Some dealers roll them back, some don't. Instead, let the general mechanical condition of the car be your guide. Forget the speedometer.

The chances are very good that you will come up with a sound automobile if you satisfy yourself with respect to the points above. To know what to look for is the first tip in protecting yourself against being taken for a ride.

5

Shopping, Negotiating, Buying

in which the dramatic arts get a workout

Now that we have come this far let us go to buy that used car. It has been mentioned that this business is akin to horse trading. What makes it so is that nine chances out of ten you are going to trade your critter for a critter the other fellow acquired in a prior trade. Trading transforms the normal retail buyer/seller relationship into a situation in which the merit of the merchandise is open to question. And this goes for both sides of the trade. It is inherent in the business. You are going to try to get as much as possible for your car; the used car salesman is going to make the best deal he can for his dealership. This is adversary vs. adversary—and that salesman is a pro, while you are an amateur.

How To Buy A Used Car

First, go shopping. One can always be a gentleman, and should be. At the same time let us not forget the truth of the phrase that "Nice guys finish last". Shopping will help to protect you and help to get you a good car. Keep in mind that it is your money that is being spent. When shopping:

DO: Go to three or four lots until you have located two to three cars that you could be seriously interested in buying. If the salesman who greets you seems to be a good Joe and helpful, ask for him if and when you return to his lot. On your initial visits state that you intend to buy within twenty-four hours but for the moment you are shopping and expect to visit other lots. Describe what you want and indicate the price range. Emphasize that car condition is more important than price. He will show cars that may be of interest but beyond giving bare information will not make a great effort to sell you (the comment that you are shopping stopped that) and no time is wasted. Fifteen minutes per lot ought to get the job done.

DO NOT: Do not spend time in price discussion and debate. Queried about the price on a specific car the usual reply to shoppers is that the asking price is $1,995 or $1,445 or whatever, sometimes with the strong implication that it might be lower if no trade-in is involved or, if there is a trade, that a generous trade-in allowance can be had. At this preliminary stage the asking price is a point of departure, not necessarily final. Exceptions would be cars advertised in a bona-fide sale, these priced at low figures in the ads to create customer traffic. Do not invite or expect to get an appraisal on your car to establish a trade-in value at this point. This would be a time waster. In fact, many dealerships and especially

Shopping, Negotiating, Buying

system houses will not make an appraisal until the deal is well advanced.

In almost any community this preliminary shopping job can be accomplished in an hour or not much more. It establishes these elements—you will have located two or three possible purchases that please you, you will know price ranges, you have emphasized car condition as more important than price. As to this last, the result is that salesmen will not show you cars in doubtful condition and will show you the cream of the stock in your price range. The final price must be negotiated in any event. Basic in this is that you have the initiative. You are buying a car and not being sold one. Your statement that you are shopping alerts salesmen to a sharply competitive situation. They will respond by eventually (eventually, mark you) offering the best deal they can.

The Negotiation: So many techniques are employed by various dealerships that it is not realistic to attempt to describe them all. "System Houses" have systematized the operation to the point where the buyer is passed from hand to hand like a partner in a square dance—from the first contact salesman known as a "liner", to appraiser, to a "closer" or sales manager, to finance man, this manipulation progressively wearing the buyer down. System houses are usually big-volume, high-pressure operators offering tremendous deals (often impossible deals when you get there) in TV and newspaper advertising. You know—practically new automobiles for $59.50 down and thirty-six trifling monthly payments. *If* the credit is good. Certainly, Rockefeller's credit is that good but not that of many others and somehow the deal changes, the customer

49

winding up with a chattel mortgage on his furniture. Old line dealerships—"straight houses"—often prefer to have experienced sales people and long-time employees, and to handle their own deals from first contact on the lot, through the appraisal, negotiation, credit statement, close and delivery of the unit. These can be big or little dealers. They all hate system houses like poison because the unrealizeable "come-on" offers in system house advertising do lead people to believe that they can buy expensive cars for little down and practically forever to pay.

However, you cannot know what system is being used by an individual dealer—indeed, many have no system at all. This is about the way it will go, depending on the type of operation. Your one-hour shopping action will have located two or three suitable cars. Focus on the one that you believe is best. Tell the salesman you are going to buy at once and that you are there to do business if the deal is satisfactory. Don't be coy about this. The industry is plagued by people who go to used car lots to kick tires. These characters have no intention of buying but are spending idle hours. They have no compunction about asking a multitude of questions and wasting the time of all concerned. If they tried that with an attorney or a doctor it would get them a bill for professional advice.

Anyway, you ask for the price of the car, and you are told. Incidentally, I have known used car managers (lazy) who issued stock sheets all too infrequently and pretty much left it up to the salesman to use his own judgment as to how much to ask. The commission being a percentage of the gross profit the salesman is going to try for all the traffic will bear. It gives him room to maneuver.

Shopping, Negotiating, Buying

By this time the price of the dealer's car has been quoted and the trade-in appraised. What now takes place is a short theater skit involving two or three actors in a number of scenes. It is a necessary routine, varied from time to time according to the temperament of the buyer, the techniques of the salesmen, and whatever system, if any at all, is employed by the dealership.

Before we get into the skit let it again be commented that dealers would like few things better than to be able to establish fixed prices on the used cars they offer, and give a once and final offer for the trade. Fixed prices are a commonplace in every other field of retailing. But it is not a commonplace in the used car business. The buyer himself will not permit it. He is not only buying a car but also selling one—trading. And this is *the* complicating factor.

Generally, the negotiating skit follows a pattern something like this:

HERMAN BIGHEART, the salesman: "Mr. Olson, the price on that creampuff of a DeLuxe Appalachian four door is $1,895. Let's see, your Pumpernickel Special is appraised at $550 so that makes a difference of $1,345 plus sales tax and transfer of title. What do you say—shall we write it up?" Herman is quoting the appraiser's figure establishing the wholesale value of the trade-in, and has just hurled what is known as the "low ball." This is shock treatment, a way to bring the customer down to earth about the real value of his trade. And it opens the door for serious bargaining.

OLE OLSON, the buyer: "What! Pumpernickels not as good as mine are selling on lots all over town for $750

How To Buy A Used Car

and better. And just a couple of months ago I bought a new battery and had a new muffler installed. Oh, yes, and a new water pump three or four months ago, too." (This work was performed well over a year ago—but never mind.) "$550 is way off. I ought to get at least $700."

HERMAN the salesman: "Look, I didn't make the appraisal. It may seem low to you but honestly that's all it is worth to us. We'd just as soon have the $550 as your car." (Herman is truthful in this. The dealership would rather have the $550 than Ole's Pumpernickel.) At this stage if Herman has a copy of the appraisal form with deficiencies noted he is in a position to point out there is no spare tire, tires on the ground are bald, paint and metal work is needed on the front fenders, and so on. If he has no completed appraisal form Herman can still argue these matters but his position is weakened. Of course, Ole knows what must be done to keep the car roadable, that's why he is trading. But the form helps to bring home to Ole what is needed and that it will cost money.

HERMAN continues: "I agree that your Pumpernickel is a solid piece. But we are going to have to spend $75 or $100 to get it ready for sale; maybe more if there are other troubles. If you'll sign an order right now I'll see if I can't get you $600—I'll really try. I need the business. Okay?" And he reaches for the order pad and starts writing.

OLSON: "No, sir. I'm not going to let that good car go for any $600. My brother-in-law offered me over $700 for it just last month." (It ain't so but customers are naughty that way. His brother-in-law lives 800 miles away, hasn't seen Ole in a year, owns his own business, just bought a

Shopping, Negotiating, Buying

new Cadillac.) "Besides, I want to be certain about the condition of that car I'm interested in. I'd like to take it to a mechanic friend of mine."

HERMAN: "Why, go ahead and take it. Keep it three or four hours. Get it back here before we close though; the house doesn't want cars out overnight. Leave the Pumpernickel here and I'll have it checked out again. If I can get that appraisal raised to $650 and maybe get the manager to cut the price on our car, you might come out with the $700 you want."

In his last remark Herman Bigheart has demonstrated that the dramatic arts may have lost a competent actor. He has skillfully thrown what is known as the "high-ball" to the departing Ole; this being an offer so generous that Olson is taken out of the market where competitor dealers are concerned. The high-ball will bring Olson back without his detouring to shop elsewhere. Even if he does shop, he will not commit himself. Meantime, Herman has said that he will try for $700—this does not mean that surely he will be successful in getting the $700.

Another matter: Ole may stop at his home to show the car to his wife. It will be in his driveway in a familiar setting, it is such an improvement over what the family has been driving that his wife will approve even though she might prefer a sort of, you know, off-white color instead of that light blue. His neighbor will admire it and say so. Ole is unconsciously making a commitment.

Ole takes the car to his neighborhood auto repair shop where they have been taking care of the Pumpernickel. The owner is a good mechanic, a former service manager for a big dealer until he opened his own plant. He checks

How To Buy A Used Car

out the car and pronounces it to be in fairly sound shape. And here we point a moral: When Ole first went shopping he stated that the car he wanted had to be in good mechanical condition and that this was the most important consideration. As a result Bigheart showed him the best cars on the lot and steered him away from others that may have looked as good but that he, good old Herman Bigheart, suspected might be wanting mechanically. I mention that when Ole took the car to the neighborhood shop for inspection he did tell them he was thinking of buying it; he did not say where it was from.

Now if this simple inspection seems a lot of bother, bear in mind that the action should not take over an hour or so and should not cost over $5 to $7.50. Isn't it to safeguard a $1,895 expenditure? If we could count on the dealers making thorough inspections when they service the car for the front line, inspection by an outsider wouldn't be necessary—but we cannot count on the dealers for that, most of them. However, few people act to get this protection when they buy a used car. And to give them their due, dealers have no objection to an outside inspection and are cheerful about it when it is suggested.

OLSON returns: "The car seems pretty good. But the bumper jack is missing and so's the cigarette lighter. The spare tire is a dog. If you'll get those things taken care of, I might deal. But not at $600 for my Pumpernickel. No, Sirree."

HERMAN: (he's been through this countless times.) "Well, I said I'd try to get you a better allowance on your trade. How much do you have to have?"

OLSON: "I want $700 or no dice."

Shopping, Negotiating, Buying

HERMAN: "Brother, that's a load. But if I don't sell cars I don't eat. The inventory is high now and maybe the house will relax and give on this." Herman is now on Olson's side, and as a friend is conspiring with Ole to force the house into a better deal. "I'll write up an order. I'll have to have a deposit. I can take jawbone orders to the sales manager all day long and he won't even listen. But a signed order and a deposit—say $20 as earnest money—is different. If he okays the deal, you've bought the car." And Herman writes the order allowing $700 for the Pumpernickel. Ole signs it and produces the $20.

BIGHEART goes to Eli Scrooge, the sales manager: "The radio in the closing room on the lot just said that Willie Mays busted a homer a couple of minutes ago. Anyway, I got a write-up here on that blue 1964 DeLuxe Appalachian. The trade is appraised at $550 and the write-up is for $700 allowance. The buyer's name is Olson and his credit looks real good. What say?"

SCROOGE: "Don't you guys ever turn off that radio? Instead of listening to it you'd be better off lining up those cars. That lot is a mess. Okay. Tell him $650 for his trade. That's a $100 up. But don't lose him."

BIGHEART back to Olson: "I really worked him over but he wouldn't hold still for that $700 allowance. Now look here, I've got to sell a car today. It's been a bad week and I'm willing to try him again at $675. But that's the last. How about it? That's really a good car and a good deal." Olson agrees and is secretly delighted. He was actually willing to close for the $650 but couldn't bring himself to say so, Herman didn't stay with it long enough. Too, Olson is just about worn out.

How To Buy A Used Car

BIGHEART to Scrooge: "Got the deal for $675 allowance for the Pumpernickel. This Olson is a tough trader. Okay?"

SCROOGE: "Still giving the joint away are you? Okay, I'll accept it. Tell him he can have the Appalachian tomorrow if his credit checks out. Check the credit statement yourself. And see if you can get a little more money than the $20 you are holding. I don't want him to get buyer's remorse. You never know until the tail light is over the curb."

Now what is the foregoing rigamarole all about? Is this sort of thing realistic? It is somewhat more elaborate than the average negotiation—but the basics are there. Proposals and counter-proposals until a meeting place is found. There are many, many salesmen who want to handle their customers all the way, without going through anyone else—do their own appraising and close their own deals. This is a matter of pride and they want no part of any such charade. Other salesmen want help very early in the selling operation and they need it. Some dealerships do not want men who cannot close without help, others introduce closing specialists into the negotiation as a matter of course.

For myself, I feel that the manager should occasionally have his place in helping to complete the sale. The presence of the third party can have its effect. Again, on the matter of price and profit it is the manager who can make an immediate decision that the inventory is too high and reduce it by this sale anyway; or, that since the month-end inventory and sales report to the factory is due day

Shopping, Negotiating, Buying

after tomorrow the deal should be made to help make the sales figures look better.

As for Olson, the tough trader: He got a good car by 1) insisting at the outset that he wanted a sound automobile and had no interest in anything else, and 2) having it checked out for mechanical condition, which few people do, and 3) got $125 over wholesale for his Pumpernickel. Granted, the price of the Appalachian was $100 high to allow for trading. But not $125. Olson's time was worth more than the $25 he saved and the three hours it took for him to locate and buy the car but, after all, he was spending $1,895 and he got the car he wanted, a *good* one.

Now then, lets run a critique on the above negotiation. In a preceding chapter there was warning to keep the money difference in mind—the difference in money between the allowance for the trade and the price of the car Olson was purchasing. It seems to me that Olson focused most of his attention on what he was going to get for his trade-in and forgot all about the price of the car he was getting. True enough, that's about the average buyer's attitude. He wasn't hurt however since at the beginning he emphasized car condition over price and as a result was shown only good cars and settled on one of these. And he ensured that it was a sound car by having a qualified man inspect it for brakes, steering, and general performance.

Remember our little tale about Joe and Harriet? They were so impressed by Brown's deal when he offered them an extra hundred for *their* Pumpernickel (and the extra hundred was in the asking price on the one they bought) that they left themselves wide open to be sold a car that might have been rough. The salesman said it was a good car but with a lot of salesmen all the cars in stock are good. But Brown is a good dealer and he does not handle any bum iron—he dumps rough cars retail or wholesale at give-away prices in consideration of their condition. But you must admit he knows how to sell the good ones. So Joe and Harriet got a good car. Joe was vulnerable for a while. He doesn't know as much about cars as he thinks he does.

Where is dealer Green in all this? Remember, his salesman lost Joe to dealer Brown. He has hiked his asking prices $100, is giving this away in overallowances, and has quit losing deals.

What of Aunt Agatha and Uncle Charley? Everyone says they are such *nice* people. And they are too. They, unlike Olson the tough customer, might not get a $675 allowance for their old Pumpernickel. But—nice guys do win ball games some times! Dealers are just as good people as there are in any given community. In many ways so are the used car salesmen, too, and having been one of the breed I'm qualified to say. But the salesman's job is to sell any and all used cars on the lot. The more experienced salesmen do not *sell* cars; they let people *buy* them in the sense that if a prospect likes and finally settles on a car, the salesman will have little comment to make about the merit of the unit but let the buyer sell himself, the salesman winding up the deal during the negotiation. He will give as good a deal as the buyer can get out of him. But it is remembered that his wage is probably based on a percentage of the gross (the spread between cost of the unit to the dealer and the selling

Shopping, Negotiating, Buying

price) and he has three times the incentive to go for a $300 gross than he has for a $100 gross. Some salesmen will be easy on Aunt Agatha and Uncle Charley—and some won't.

But if Aunt Agatha and Uncle Charley state at the outset that good condition in the car they want to buy is paramount they'll wind up with a good car and, probably, $650 for their faithful old Pumpernickel. Their chances of doing so might be helped if they read this book.

I say again, and again, that dealers would like nothing better than to be able to post firm, unalterable prices on the cars they sell, and offer firm, unalterable allowances for the cars they must take in trade. But the public won't let them. It seems that everybody has a brother-in-law like Olson's who is eager to give Olson $700, maybe $750, for that Pumpernickel instead of what the dealer offers. Why won't the public let the dealer's salesmen just state fair and reasonable prices on his individual cars? Reflect: Dealer Green tried it. But Joe and Harriet who explored the matter and listened to Green's salesman went on to Dealer Brown who convinced them that he was offering a better car (because it was higher priced). Besides, he was so much more appreciative of the really fine Pumpernickel Joe and Harriet had to trade that he was quite willing to give a better allowance.

It should be noted that the dealer is not alone in having faults. The used car buyer has been known to have a few. Somehow or other, the buying public often assigns liberties to itself that would be unforgiveable in a dealer. Some people, learning that the transmission is gone on their car, or the rear end, or that the frame is out of line, will hightail it for a dealership and start trading. In the process they forget to mention what's wrong with their cars. After the first hard freeze of the year, there are always a few unfortunates who have failed to put in antifreeze. The result is a cracked block so they tell the mechanic to put on a new head gasket and button up the engine. They go trading, a lapse of memory interfering with a candid explanation as to what happened to the engine.

Dealers will not knowingly sell cars with major defects; when troubles are discovered on any unit better than an absolute junker they will repair or rebuild to correct it. The difficulty is that few dealers follow a policy of inspection and test for every incoming trade. The attitude with the majority seems to be "Why look for trouble?"

6

Used Car Financing

in which Hector V. Throckmorton buys a car he cannot afford and is shown the mousehouse technique, and Elmer Gayboy has marital troubles

All of us know that the great majority of used cars are sold on the installment plan. Not so many years ago financing was simple and straightforward, fair to the customers and to those doing the financing. But in the past fifteen years and more of unprecedented boom in the economy there has been a sad deterioration of credit standards. Also—entry into the installment finance business has been made by some unsound, risky, and just plain usurious practitioners.

Use care in financing the car you buy; not to do so could be very expensive. Before you sign an order make certain that you know what the finance charge is going to be. More than 33 states have laws restricting the

Used Car Financing

amounts that can be charged for auto financing but even in these states the maximum may be, in some instances, awfully high. The maximum permitted is geared to cover poor-risk credit with the result that rates are high. About fifteen states have no auto finance laws at all. Illinois has no such law protecting car buyers. In that state in March of 1966, a man walked into a finance company with a shotgun and, fortunately, blasted it only into the ceiling. He had paid $600 down on a car having a price tag of $2,200, signed up for payments of $97 per month for 30 months. The day came when he couldn't pay and the finance company took the car away. And they told him he still owed $1,300. His $600 down payment was gone. And his car was gone. And he still owed the $1,300. He had been taken for a total purchase, car plus finance charge, plus state tax, amounting to $3,510—a 60% finance charge! Also, in Illinois, in January, 1966, a man walked into a dealership and, enraged about his financing, shot two men to death with a shotgun. One must suspect that he was deranged; he might have done much the same to others in a totally different situation and for other causes. But it was done. I do not have facts about the details in this last case—but there it is, to ponder. Some of these loan companies "play" rough. And they get a lot of cooperation from dealers who write their (financing) paper. The majority of dealers will not stoop to this sort of thing—but a lot of them still overdo it.

Your credit union is a good place to finance your car; so is the bank on a direct loan; so are the finance companies owned by the car manufacturers. And there are other good finance outfits. Still, on the other side of the coin, there are plenty of gougers. To protect yourself, insist on knowing what the finance charge is. And what the finance charge *rate* is; that is, is it 7% or 8½% or what? Find out what it is on an annual basis. Have the salesman show you how he arrived at his figures. One would think that all car buyers are financial wizards and geniuses in arithmetic according to the way they agree with the seller on these charges when presented during the sale. You'd think they had been doing the sums in their heads. Actually, few buyers know how much they are paying for financing their installment payments, or the rate on which the charges are being based while the deal is being negotiated. And does the salesman tell them what rate is being used? No! Ask for the finance details—it is your money that the salesman is helping you to spend. You have a right to know, and you should be smart enough to ask!

There is a difference, too, between finance *charges* and finance *interest* but we'll come to that a little later.

A guideline on how to finance your used car transaction is to buy a car whose price is low enough to permit you to pay at least 30% as down payment including sales tax and motor vehicle department fees. Buying used cars on a low down payment basis, say 5% or 10% down on the total cost of the transaction, can set you up for very high cost finance charges.

Following are examples of what every used and new car salesman sees once or twice a week, perhaps oftener. Can you see yourself in one of these vignettes?

Hector V. Throckmorton has come into the dealership and is about to buy a new car, or a quality used car. A stage is reached where the salesman hauls out the credit application form and informs Hector that he is going to ask some personal questions. Hector, accustomed to this

Used Car Financing

interrogation since he has been through it many times, comes up with the data on his age, where he lives, where he is working and for how long, the amount of his take-home pay, the names of three pals whom he is sure will say he is a fine citizen and no burglar (burglars pay cash). "Are you married? How many children?" Hector obliges; he is married, has three children. Now a moment of truth. "Where do you bank?" It seems that Hector has a checking account but no savings account. His checking account has an average balance of $150 according to Hector. (Actually, the account balance is $20 as of the moment and not often, in fact rarely, is as high as $150). "Where have you credit and amounts outstanding?" In the end, it appears that Hector has a take-home pay of $112.50 per week, owes on the TV, has a house mortgage, is paying off a $350 personal loan entered into when the family drove to Nebraska to visit his wife's mother last July, and owes an $80 balance on an outboard engine he bought on half-share with a friend who owns a boat. Also, there are two department store bills. He has forgotten that he still owes installments on the washing machine and drier, and owes the hospital a little on the delivery of the last child because he failed to join the group health insurance available where he works. It is now apparent that Hector is hurting financially. But more! He still owes 7 payments on his car, having bought this 17 months ago with 24 monthly payments. It is a reasonably good car, a little rough, but his equity is worth $225. He has no cash to go with it. He wants the pay-off made by the dealer as part of the transaction on the car he is buying today. He is trying to buy a car selling for $1,945. Obviously enough, not a new car.

How To Buy A Used Car

Now is the time for the salesman to come up with a stern Dutch Uncle routine. It can be pointed out to Hector that his present car is big enough for the family, seems solid enough, and that while it needs new tires, a new battery, probably a brake job, $20 worth of metal work on the front fender and a complete tune-up, this could all be handled for not over $120. Further, the dealer would be glad to handle it for 12 payments of $12 per month or maybe less depending on the bill.

Does the salesman go into this Dutch Uncle routine? Probably not. Why not? First, Hector wouldn't react to this maneuver. He wants a top car in his driveway, partly to impress his neighbor who has just purchased a new Super-Goliath DeLuxe hard top, two door, with an engine almost big enough (even though it is a popular-priced car) to power a locomotive, and partly because Hector's wife, now that the oldest girl is in school, wants to attend the PTA meetings and would be embarrassed to drive up in their present five-year old car. However, Hector doesn't reveal these motivations for wanting a newer, expensive car. He has convinced himself that if he does put $85 or, worse, as much as $120 into his present car, it would be money down the drain since the older it gets the less it is worth. The trouble is that he forgets—he *wants* to forget—that if he spends $120 on putting his present car in first class condition it will give him another two years of good, safe operation. He will take less of a loss on depreciation since this will slow down from $400 or more a year on a nearly new car to perhaps $150 a year as the car gets older. The insurance is less. He is paying a lot less in finance charges. The state motor vehicle department fees are less. Then, when the

Used Car Financing

car is paid off he can trade, a year or two years from now. Is Hector impressed? Not at all. First, nobody gives him this routine. Almost no dealers, small town perhaps excepted, have any sort of policy or system about using it. The salesman isn't going to sell the idea. To begin with, he has no incentive to do so. He also guesses that Hector will walk away if he tries it. He's right, Hector will walk.

After all, the salesman is there to sell cars. He muses that while there isn't enough for a legitimate down payment after the pay-off has been made on Hector's present car contract, still and all, this guy has worked for Zilch Horgentorgal, Inc. for seven years, seems reliable, and is a little short of cash. To himself, he says sympathetically —"but who isn't short of cash?"

The salesman, to Hector: "The down payment is very short. We like to get at least $600 down on a car in the $1,945 bracket. But maybe I can fix it. How would you like to make the payments a little faster the first year to catch up on the short down payment? To make it easy let's say you pay $38.50 the first of each month for 12 months and pay $68.50 the fifteenth of each month for 24 months. You see, this'll split your payments each month so that it won't strain you to handle them. Of course, after the first 12 months you'll only have that one monthly payment. Besides, we'll pay off the balance on your present car and that is out of the way for you. What do you say?" Hector really wants that $1,945 beauty. He says "yes." He is told that the salesman is going to see if he can get the deal arranged. He is told to come back tomorrow.

Now the outcome of all this depends on the type of

How To Buy A Used Car

dealer. Remember, Hector's present car on which he still owes seven payments is worth enough above the balance still owed on the contract so that the dealer can make the pay-off and still give Hector a $225 credit as cash towards his down payment. Let's say the car is worth $625 wholesale, the pay-off is $400. That leaves the dealer a $625 car (wholesale) to put in stock after the $400 pay-off and $225 to Hector.

Hector is now on the verge of making a $2,030.80 purchase but he doesn't know it. It works out this way: the car he is buying is $1,945, sales tax is $77.80, transfer of registration is $8.00—total $2,030.80. What about the financing?

It depends on the dealership. Hector has his credit strained to the limit. There is no reserve for contingencies. But he has a solid job, held for seven years. Having three children and a wife he is pretty well draft proof. Being of the recent breed, installment payments do not scare him.

If the dealer is willing to take the risk and gamble (in the new economics they call it forward looking and progressive) he'll okay the deal. The bank or finance company where the dealer does business will lend wholesale (low book) value, plus sales tax and registration fees. The amount they are willing to lend is several hundred short of the selling price. So the dealer gambles that Hector will pay—if he doesn't his $225 down is considered as rent—if he doesn't pay off like a clock, back comes the car.

Just as likely however is the probability that Hector has been set up for what is called "mousehousing". Perhaps the dealer is the old fogey type who believes that people shouldn't buy what they cannot really afford, and

Used Car Financing

doesn't like to gamble. But he does like to sell cars. The salesman then will take the credit application to a "Mousehouse"—a personal loan company—to see if he can get them to agree to write a one year contract for $400 plus a finance charge of $62 for a total of $462. The dealership gets the $400. Hector pays $38.50 per month for 12 months to pay off the personal loan—payments the first of every month remember. Finance *charge* on this is 15%. The other monthly payment of $68.50 is a finance *charge* of 7½% per annum, for two years, to be paid on the 15th of each month.

Having done his spadework the salesman presents Hector with two contracts when he returns. One of these is from the loan company which wants collateral for the $400 loan. Their contract contains a chattel mortgage on Hector's furniture. Two financing agencies, two contracts, both mortgages on Hector's goods. The salesman has not informed Hector that the split payments involved two contracts but when Hector sees they are substantially what he expected to pay each month in two separate payments he goes along with the deal and proudly drives that $1,945 "creampuff" home. His Super Goliath-owning neighbor can see that there is no dust on Hector, and Hector's wife can drive to the PTA meetings in calm confidence that her personal transportation meets the standards of that elevated body. In sober fact Hector's neighbor couldn't care less, and the PTA people wouldn't pay any attention unless Mrs. Hector arrived on a skateboard.

This mousehousing tactic seems absurd but it does take place a surprising number of times. An alarming number of times. I think it is because almost two generations of customers, blessed be their tribe, have grown up to believe

How To Buy A Used Car

in confidence that instant credit was invented to be used and that they are not going to have any problem meeting the installment obligations.

If there is any moral to this story let it be that all of the Hectors should avoid buying used cars on which they cannot make a down payment of at least 30%, cash or trade or both, and this includes taxes and license plates and transfer. Hector should have waited, made the seven remaining payments on his car, bought the tires, battery and brakes it needed, and driven it for another year or more. Then, if all *does not* go well with him financially, for whatever reason, he will not be in a financially overextended position. If all *does* go well, he can then buy a 1966 or 1967 model rather than the 1965 he was trying for.

A reverse situation sometimes, but infrequently, presents itself. Occasionally, a buyer will show up with an ample down payment for a used car. In checking his credit application the finance company reports that the prospective credit is simply lousy and that they don't want the paper but will lend low book wholesale if the paper is endorsed (guaranteed) by the dealer. If the dealer's manager is willing to gamble, since there is a substantial down payment, he will tell the salesman, "okay, roll that car. If the buyer doesn't pay we'll consider the down payment as rent and get the car back." Salesmen bless these managers and know when a case fits house policy. Other dealers want no part of this type of business; the salesman then knows that the finger is pointed at the no sale key on the cash register unless he can find a more liberal finance company (with higher rates considering it is risky business) to handle the deal.

Used Car Financing

As a result of this mousehousing every experienced salesman, particularly in metropolitan industrial areas, frequently meets visitors to his lot who are driving cars they want to trade, the cars generally being in sorry condition although not necessarily old. Salesmen learn to "qualify" customers in a hurry. They soon learn if the trade-in still has a balance due against it and how much. It can develop that the car might have a value of $600 and be in hock to the finance companies for over $1,500. I have experienced this. Since it is manifestly almost impossible for a car to be financed so far over its current value, the would-be buyer will admit that he had to hock his furniture to buy the car. This man is in trouble. He cannot walk away from the car. Even if no other chattel mortgage is involved the disparity between the car value and the balance due can be such that when the finance company gets the car back they will sue for a deficiency judgment. And he will have lost the car and the furniture and still owe money.

Truth to tell, people who get into this sort of situation are usually such poor prospects for further collection that the finance companies may let matters slide rather than involve themselves in additional red tape and expense.

Here is something that few people seem to know. The cost of financing is usually expressed as the finance "charge." It is not expressed as interest although most people seem to regard it as such. The state of California quite rightly makes every car sales order show the exact and total amount charged for financing. The order may not be signed by the customer in blank and his copy, signed by an agent of the dealer, is presented to him at the time the deal is concluded. Thus the customer is informed in writing, as shown on the order, of the details of the transaction, including a statement of the amount of the finance charge.

Why "charges" instead of "interest"? A 6% finance charge is actually between 11% and 12% interest per year, the reason being that it is paid on the full amount for a period of a year while the balance diminishes because of payments each month. Put simply, the customer is paying 6% per annum on, say, $1,000 the first month; however, with every month that passes the balance owed is reduced until on the last month he owes only one twelfth of the amount originally borrowed but is still paying a finance charge at the rate of 6% on the original full $1,000 amount. But do not get the idea that it is only 6% interest —it is not. It is a finance charge that actually amounts to slightly less than 12% interest.

New cars are usually sold financed at 6% finance charge per annum, the 6% multiplied by the number of years the contract will run. As an illustration: if the new car is delivered on a contract calling for 36 monthly installments, the finance charge is 18% of the amount financed (6% for each contract year, times 3 years). It is not too much, is fair, and the buyer's credit must be good to obtain it. The risk to the financing agency is higher in the case of used cars so that finance charges, depending on customer credit, for cars one year old might be 7½%, two-year old-cars 8½%, three-year-old cars from there on up. Usually, one-year-old cars will not be financed for over 30 months, two year old cars for 24 months, and older cars for 18 months or less.

One frequently sees newspaper advertisements inserted by banks offering to finance cars for a $4.50 or $5.00 finance charge per $100 per year. This rate would apply

Used Car Financing

only to new cars. With good credit on the part of the customer a $6.00 per year per $100 rate might be had on a recent used car. Fair enough. The bank may be paying 4½% interest on the savings of their depositor, i.e. $45 per year for $1,000 of deposit for the full year. Since their finance charge is $6.00 per hundred per year they are actually getting about 11½% interest (slightly more) since the diminishing balance feature must be taken into account. In other words what they are buying for $45 they are selling for $115—not a bad gross profit. What the bank is concerned about is not the gross profit, but the net profit. From the gross they must deduct what it costs to administer clerical overhead, the cost of investigating credit applications, handle collections, and in the case of loans that have turned out badly, the losses. Finance is always a matter of relative risk for the man or institution that loans the money. Looking at it from the viewpoint of the lender, how many people would be willing to lend $2,000 to a comparative stranger in the hope of getting it back at the end of two years. Consider the risk and the work involved. So there it is. This type of rate is available only from banks making the loan *directly* to customers whose credit reliability has been well checked out.

Occasionally one sees advertisements and dealer statements to the effect that they give bank rates. In general this means that they have good bank connections and keep reserve funds on deposit in those banks to cover the dealer's endorsement of the customer's contract. The contract is put through the bank, it is the bank's money that is being used and the monthly payments are made to the bank or to the dealer. But it does not follow that the customer is getting a low bank rate—his finance charge is whatever the dealer has put on the contract. The dealer has endorsed the installment paper to the bank, in consequence the bank is entirely protected against loss and gives the money to the dealer at a low rate, the dealer taking the difference. Under the terms of this financing it is the dealer who must take back the car in the case of repossession (this is known as recourse), must pay off the outstanding balance due the bank and take whatever loss there may be on the car.

It may be appropriate to add here that repossessions are at an all-time low as a result of booming times and high employment. For the big conservative financing agencies such as the credit institutions owned and operated by the car manufacturers, repos are running at something like one quarter of one percent. This is because they require an adequate down payment and will not approve contracts with bad credit risks. Out of every four hundred car sales that they finance one may become a repossession. Three hundred and ninety nine cars are paid off. The risk is minimal the way they run the business, so losses are minimal. They can afford to give, and do give, fair rates to people who buy from their dealers. One of their objectives is to retain the good will of the public who buy the cars produced by the auto manufacturers who also own and control the lending institution. My experience with these big outfits is that their rates are no more than need be to operate a conservative business, their profit is reasonable, they understand borrowers and their problems and treat them with consideration and fairness. If a man has been ill or had other hard luck (and that doesn't include losing the last two months payments in a dice game) they will listen to reason and grant a postponement or an extension of payments on a refinanced basis. It is also to be commented that their experience with human beings is vast and profound; they have myriad times heard all the excuses for non-payment that imaginative individuals could invent. They are not easily "conned". In essence, they do want their money; they do not want the car. However, to lend money and not ever get it or the security back is no way "to run an airline". You wouldn't do business on that basis either if you could help it—always excepting the $200 your wife's brother borrowed from you last year and that really couldn't be helped.

Here are some odd lots about how financing ties into used car sales. Any number of people, maybe millions, have a rather vague idea that buying a repossessed car is to get a bargain. No! It definitely is not. If Harry, who works where you do, is quitting to go to Nova Scotia and wants to get rid of his car on which there are 15 payments due (and wants $200 for his equity) that's another matter—Harry is selling his car and is about to transfer the finance contract. But repossessions are made by dealers or finance companies only as a last resort; when cars are repossessed the owners have generally let them go without maintenance for so long they are not worth anywhere near the balance due the finance company. If the car has a value equal to the finance balance against it, the owner can almost always sell it before the finance company comes around. If a man is forced to miss a payment or two, his best course is go and explain the matter to the finance people—he'll find them receptive and understanding if he is truthful. As previously stated however, they have heard all the stories and cannot be taken in by fairy tales.

One sees an increasing number of advertisements stating

that all the buyer need do is pay a salesman's fee of $25 dollars and one or two monthly payments, assume the balance and drive the car away. The implication is that this is a liquidation of repossessions providing an opportunity to take advantage of some other guy's distress and loss. It arises since there is this widespread belief that repos are bargains. Don't you believe it. If tempted, find out about the finance charges. Be doubly sure about the financing in the event that the required down payment is less than 20% of the cost of the car.

I can recall one used car operator who had a different way of doing things. He put good cars, in sound condition and attractive, on his lot at practically wholesale prices. They were absolute bargains at the windshield posted prices where cash buyers were concerned. But we know that nine out of ten buyers have a trade-in. Buyers would come in, be delighted with car and price, then scream to the skies when told the allowance for the trade-in. They would be told that the dealer's cars were absolute bargains at the quoted prices, which was completely true; that the trade-in was worth no more than what had been offered but they might increase the offer, and this was true; that the operation was one aimed to sell as many cars as possible at down to earth prices, which was also true. Customers were urged to walk out and shop other lots and then come back if they hadn't bought in the meantime. Many did come back. Now, how can a used car operator make money selling his merchandise at wholesale? For what the car cost him plus his cost of repair and readying for sale? He cannot, if that is all there is to it. The little addition was a finance contract that reached

Used Car Financing

the upper limits in finance charges. This didn't have a startling effect on each monthly payment over the spread of 18 to 24 months—but that is where the profit was. And there was a provision in the contract preventing premature payment of the contract with recapture of any part of the financing charge. Now all this sounds like duplicity and that the operator was a bad boy, indeed. Not altogether. The dealer's cars were good, sound, and priced at the absolute rock bottom. He offered as much for trade-ins as they were worth and often more. He gave excellent guarantees and after-delivery service to his customers, being more than generous in this respect. But you cannot run a business without a profit and he took his profit entirely out of the financing whereas he might have tried, as do most dealers, to make most on the car and less on the finance paper. The operation was a reversal of the usual approach of pricing cars to leave room for a discount or an over-allowance. Being unusual, it worked.

Some of the big volume system houses put out hysterical, frantic, carnival-type advertising telling the public to come in, "We're open 'till ten o'clock every night. Even if you live fifty miles away it's worth the drive to save hundreds of dollars". The ads offered brand new or nearly new cars at what seemed to be below dealer cost. "This beautiful, brand new, current model lists at $3,149. It can be yours for only $2,395. Drive it away on approved credit." With motor vehicle department fees, sales tax, and finance charges, that car is going to cost $3,472.37 at the very least before it is paid for. For one thing, the ad does not state that the monthly payments will be for 48 months.

How To Buy A Used Car

For another, "approved credit" means that the man who goes to that dealer hoping to get this beauty for a mere $67.93 down and drive it away is going to have to have collateral besides the car. If he has an equity of $3,000 or $4,000 in his house he will be asked to sign a "home owners loan" which will be a trust deed or second mortgage. The car is still a chattel. The other collateral protects the selling dealer against whatever loss may be incurred if the car, after repossession, does not bring the amount of the balance owed. And it won't either. Or the deal could include a mousehouse chattel on the furniture.

You hear the home owners loan finance companies touted quite a bit. The *minimum* interest is just a trifle shy of 13%—that's on personal loans. Often it is far more. The householder's equity in his home is the security. For the man who must have the money it is a welcome service. But expensive.

This is a roughly competitive business and dealers do what they must to sell their cars. We previously discussed the sad deterioration of credit standards. The dealer is in the position with finance companies of having to endorse installment paper for recourse. The finance companies will seldom accept low down-payment paper without recourse, the dealer guaranteeing to the finance company that he will be responsible for payment in the event the buyer falls down on his obligation. Customers, many of them, insist on buying $2,000 cars and expect to do it with, say, a $200 down payment. If one dealer does not oblige then another will. A dealer must take the risk from time to time. Since it is a big risk that he can avoid only by mousehousing with a second finance company, he may

Used Car Financing

instead choose to make himself liable for losses. In which event, the higher the risk, the higher the finance charge, so dealers charge plenty on these short down deals. We've said this before but it bears repeating.

As to banks, many do the bulk or all of their car financing with the car dealers and insist on the recourse clause. With many banks, if an individual's credit is good enough to get a direct loan on a car purchase, with the car as collateral, it will be almost good enough to get the loan without security. Which means the credit must be good, indeed. It is the reverse of the coin: low risk, low charges.

The following has to do with "cheapies." Old cars getting towards the end of their economic life are not worth much—but they are worth something. Most eight, nine, and ten-year-old cars, and some even older, have a useful service life remaining that can amount to three or more years. Others in this age bracket should go straight to the junk dealer. The older they get and the more miles they have rolled inevitably puts these aging vehicles into an increasingly dubious position with regard to condition. While their selling price will not justify costly reconditioning—an engine rebuild, for instance, would be like putting a $300 saddle on a $75 horse—still, lots of them do have that three or four years of faithful, economic service to provide. What to do?

I applaud those legitimate dealers who advertise a clearance on old cars at low, low prices. With no guarantees. They are doing the public a favor. Their aim is not unselfish for they are trying to get rid of an accumulation of old cars that are cluttering up their lots, providing busy hours for the lot maintenance crew but just too good to justify calling in the junk man. I especially favor those

How To Buy A Used Car

honest dealer advertisers who use those wry and corny lines that go: "Madame, if you want to keep your husband home week-ends one of the following listed specials will make a good second car for him to go to work in. And he might spend Saturdays in the back yard with the car hood up, doing a little fixing."

However, most big time used car operations take the easiest way out, and maybe the most sensible too, by wholesaling their tired but still usable old iron to specialists in "cheapies". Did you know that the average car goes through five owners in its lifetime? The first owner trades it in and it goes to a second owner, two years or so afterwards it is again traded and so on, until, at shorter and shorter intervals of buying and again trading, it comes at last to rest at the end of all its journeying.

The used car dealer in the "cheapie" field is quite an operator. It is a special sort of merchandising. To begin with, he performs, though it must be said not nobly, a public service. The American public is on wheels. Students, unskilled laborers, semi-skilled and skilled workers, almost any category of both the employed and the unemployed all need automobiles. The plumber, plasterer, painter, and other aristocrats of the construction industry probably have a new model at home but they still need a second car to go to work in, perhaps at a diffcrent location every second month or so, the car to be left in the mud of a construction site, to carry tools, to sit in the rain or the snow. In other words, a good used car. The poor need a car even more. The unskilled laborer has no first car; he may alternate spells of employment with spells of unemployment; his work, when he has any, takes him ten miles north of home this month, and six miles in

Used Car Financing

the opposite direction next month, with time in between looking for another job. The cheapie operators supply the cars.

They buy them at wholesale for anywhere from $100 to $450 each. They do appearance conditioning and enough repair and fix-it work to enable the cars to start and keep running. The price is well-packed; a car worth $125 at wholesale will be priced at $345. One: this is to leave room for a trade-in over-allowance should the deal bring a trade, though the number of sales without trades in the cheapie business is much higher than normal. Two: this is a risky business incurring much loss. I will say for these dealers that they generally will give after-sale service to customers and will, within reason, try to keep his car running for him. The guarantees on cars sold are either non-existent or so vague as to be practically worthless but it is in the interest of the cheapie seller to keep the rig operating.

With regard to finance, these cars are sold by the cheapie specialist at prices far above what they cost him, and finance charges are as close to usury as the law will allow.

Most cheapies sold by the specialists are on a weekly payment basis, not on monthly payments. Unskilled laborers are often the buyers. In the main these people think in terms of weekly pay checks and $8.95 a week sounds a lot less than $38.45 a month which is the same thing. Then too, if the payment is not made promptly the cheapie operator knows it very early and can send his collector around to "rattle the tow chain" at the delinquent, this being a threat to repossess. Actually, these operators are more in the credit business than anything else. Their profits are large percentagewise, but the risks they take are large also. The buyer may be incapable of comprehending the simplest contract and unable to interpret its financial implications. He is often all too irresponsible. He is the victim of sharp practice, but the business seems to demand this in view of the risk. When life becomes boresome and fields yonder beckon, many a buyer is not hampered by a sense of obligation, and cheerfully piles himself into his car, along with his family, and disappears beyond the horizon leaving no forwarding address. The seller files a "skip" notice on him, shrugs his shoulders and continues to operate. A year later the car turns up abandoned on a side street in a town 20 miles or 2,000 miles away. The cheapie specialist may have paid $145 for the car at wholesale, put $40 in administration, overhead, and repairs into it, and perhaps collected $85 in weekly payments before the car disappeared. Originally, selling the car for $295 and a heavy load in the finance charges he had a prospective gross profit of something like $225. But, as it is, he is out $100 and he will never see the customer, the car, or the money again. He is accustomed to it. Better luck next time—it all averages out. Meantime, his collectors must be paid for they have to eat. Since rattling that tow chain requires some measure of brawn and is wearing on the nerves maybe we had better make it "eat, and drink, too."

When you see that advertisement specifying cars at so much per week you might consider the operator a public benefactor. Still, go shop a couple of other places before making a commitment. Considering his buying public, the cheapie dealer does put people in desperately needed, cheap transportation they would otherwise find most difficult or impossible to obtain.

Used Car Financing

There is one situation in which good, late model cars are repossessed. The circumstances are somewhat special. Elmer N. Gayboy, a well-loved bon vivant and man-about-town, is the proud owner of a Dazzler he purchased new six months ago for the price of $3,895 plus tax and plates. And finance charges. The car is in immaculate condition. Mr. Gayboy has been keeping up his payments, the finance balance owed against the car amounts to $2,150 or thereabouts. Mr. Gayboy wants to return the Dazzler to the dealer and take a lesser car for, say, about $600 for his equity. Why? Mr. Gayboy is not in financial difficulty at the time. At least, not yet.

The trouble is that Gayboy and his spouse are about to go into court in a divorce proceeding. Gayboy, knowledgeable by reason of his circle of friends and acquaintances, is all too aware that judges making property settlements in divorce actions could give the little woman the benefit of any doubts and among these benefits might be award of the automobile. Gayboy is apprehensive that his wife will end up with the car and he, with those monthly payments. If he loses the $650 rig in the court action, he at least is not burdened with payments on the Dazzler for the next two years.

I cannot say that this vignette has any legal justification whatever. But, infrequently, the situation arises and because people believe it is something of a solution to a special problem they do trade down trying to get out from under. The action may not have merit—but it does happen.

Incidentally, the dealer will sell the Dazzler again—at a profit.

7

A Few Odds and Ends

in which we kick around a few gripes

It has been stated that this is a unique business. I know of no other market where you can get $4,000 or $5,000 worth of merchandise for $1,995. But you can if you wisely buy a good used car. It might be three years old but it will have practically everything it had when it was new. Go buy one—if you've got the sensible down payment of 30%.

When you shop come to the point with the salesman. He will do his best to help you for he is helping himself. Don't be coy about whether you intend to buy or not. State that you are going to buy before the sun goes down, or at the latest tomorrow. But only if that would be a truthful statement.

How To Buy A Used Car

For heaven's sake, don't be a "be-back." This is the used car shopper who, having looked at a car and appearing to be on the point by buying, finally tells the salesman that he wants his wife to see it or has some other perfectly acceptable reason to go away and "be-back" another time. Trouble is that be-backs make dates to return—many a salesman has spent hours of his own time waiting for the be-back, when he otherwise would have been home or in some other pursuit of happiness and the free life. Salesman will often take a car off the front line and hide it in the shop or elsewhere, saving it for his be-back who has promised faithfully to return that evening at 7:30. There is a no-show; the salesman goes home at 9:00, cussing, and the next buyer gets rough treatment. The point is: if one makes a date to be back then either keep the date or phone to say it cannot be kept. I suspect that an excess of good manners keeps some people from being candid and the insincere "I'll be back" is an easy out.

Some customers (never you, of course) are wise guys. No matter what is offered they claim they can beat the deal. I have one friend who amused himself with these types—he'd offer a car at dealer cost, have the so confident visitor tell him he could beat it by $300 or better, then my friend would have his laugh. Don't tell the salesman what you can do—he has heard them all. Let him tell you what he will do. After he has reached a certain point he will quit giving you a quote. That does not mean that it is the best the house can and will do. But the buyer will be asked "What will you pay for the car?" If a trade is involved the question probably would be "Okay, I've said what your trade-in is worth and quoted a figure

A Few Odds and Ends

the house might accept. Now you tell me the very lowest figure you'll accept for that Pumpernickel. Maybe we can still do business. What about it?"

Seldom will a prospective buyer learn the actual selling price of the car he wants until he gets into the actual buying negotiation. This holds true for either new or used cars. Salesman just will not quote prices informally and at random. Nine out of ten times, the buyer would take his figures and go down the street shopping other dealers—running an auction so to speak. Many houses will not quote over the phone and have a policy that no shopper leaves the premises with written figures on price. And I agree with this. If you have ever been in the business you will have learned that the surest way to lose a deal is to give a final buying figure. The result is that the customer will knock your brains out by shopping the price all over town and settle with somebody else for a $10 better deal. When you find the car you want go along with the salesman and negotiate in earnest. He will try to sell you, in the end perhaps assisted by the Sales Manager. You'll get the best price possible. Then, if you refuse to sign, they'll forget you.

If a buyer is looking for a $2,000 car (pardon, $1,995) and has only 10% to put down he is kidding himself a bit unless the circumstances are most unusual. He will find dealers who will accommodate him. But he will be paying exorbitantly for the privilege.

Automobiles are no longer status symbols. If a man's car is big enough for its task and $120 for tires, battery, brakes and a tune-up will make it safe and roadable for the next two years, why spend $2,000?

I address myself especially to the very young man who

How To Buy A Used Car

has dreams of a new, low slung convertible and the girl companion to ride alongside, she being a replica of the gal in the TV Pepsi Cola commercials. If she is worth anything much she'll be just as impressed if you show up in a $300 set of wheels. Maybe more—perhaps she might get the idea that you are saving your money for a home and furniture.

I like the new car dealers as a place to buy used cars. The factories ride herd on them to operate effectively. There are a number of good independent used car dealers and when they are solid they are good places to buy. But we have said that it is hard to tell the good guys from the bad guys. This is true of new car dealers too, of course, but, in general, the new car dealer gets my vote. Find one that isn't too flamboyant in his advertising, doesn't make impossible promises, has been long established. He'll do.

For financing I like the big, old line, conservative finance organizations owned by the car manufacturers. Their rates are equitable. They treat the customers fairly. Many years ago, as I recall, the Federal government ruled against ownership and operation by car manufacturers of the automobile financing institutions. This was fought through the courts for twelve years with the result that automobile and truck producers again have major participation in the financing of their product in the retail market. This is a protection to the public and in my opinion the long court battle leading to the reversal of the ruling was in the public interest.

In connection with the above, in a sense, is the idea recurrent so often over past years that the car manufacturers should not franchise dealers, that somehow this is in

A Few Odds and Ends

restraint of trade and that discount houses should be permitted to buy cars direct from the factories, for resale. This is utter folly that opens the door wide to usurious financing. There is enough of that already, promoted by the sharks in the business. Car prices would not be less. And you can be sure that mechanical service would deteriorate. The new car dealer must make a large investment in shop equipment and parts inventory; the constant flow of service bulletins from the factory service department must be organized and used; the mechanics must be trained and kept up to the minute on servicing the product. For any make of car when a new yearly model is introduced, servicing changes and modifications occur dozens of times during the first year or so.

The new car dealer having a big investment in his business is entitled to protection and the car franchise provides that. It is time tested and it works. It is in the interest of all concerned—the public, the dealer and the car manufacturer. Never fear, any dealer has plenty of competition from other dealers representing other makes of cars and for that matter from dealers selling his own make of car. There is no restraint of trade here.

There may be times when you have become negative about buying a used car. Don't be. The three paramount matters to determine in buying your used car are probably condition, price, and finance charges. As to condition, you now know how to ensure that the car you want is sound mechanically. As to price, bear in mind that the average used car on the lot is priced to permit a hefty gross profit at that price. The dealer is prepared and willing to shave his price considerably. As to finance, find out how much the charge is, and the per annum rate (7%, 9%, 12% or whatever). If you've read this book you'll have the know-how.

This is, in the end, a good market for the used car buyer. He can get that $4,000 car (price when new) for around $1,995 or less when it is three years old. And it will have all the speed, the riding comfort, the power, the style and appeal it had when it was new, or almost all, with perhaps 80,000 miles and eight to ten years of service life remaining. Or, for that matter, one can buy a car for $300 that still has two to four years of service in prospect.

I hope this has helped. Go buy that car. Ninety-nine out of one hundred you'll be happy you did. You have seldom been offered better odds.